# OREGON

*The Beaver State*

### BY
## JOHN HAMILTON

**Abdo & Daughters**
An imprint of Abdo Publishing | abdopublishing.com

**abdopublishing.com**

Published by ABDO Publishing, a division of ABDO, PO Box 398166, Minneapolis, Minnesota 55439. Copyright © 2017 by Abdo Consulting Group, Inc. International copyrights reserved in all countries. No part of this book may be reproduced in any form without written permission from the publisher. ABDO & Daughters™ is a trademark and logo of ABDO Publishing.

Printed in the United States of America, North Mankato, Minnesota.
062016
092016

**Editor:** Sue Hamilton       **Contributing Editor:** Bridget O'Brien
**Graphic Design:** Sue Hamilton
**Cover Art Direction:** Candice Keimig   **Cover Photo Selection:** Neil Klinepier
**Cover Photo:** iStock
**Interior Images:** Alamy, AP, Dan & Linda Dzurisin, Dreamstime, Evergreen Aviation & Space Museum, Getty Images, Granger Collection, HarperCollins Publishers, Henk Rayer, Historic Naval Ships Association, History in Full Color-Restoration/Colorization, Independence National Historical Park/Artist C.W. Peale, iStock, Jacobolus, James Beard Foundation/Dan Wynn, Library of Congress, Marcus Gheeraerts, Mile High Maps, Minden Pictures, Mountain High Maps, National Archives & Records, Nike, New York Public Library, One Mile Up, Oregon Ducks, Oregon Museum of Science and Industry, Oregon State Beavers, Port of Portland, Portland Thorns, Portland Timbers, Portland Trail Blazers, Rick Leche, Science Source, Sidney Bell, Wark Photography, Wikimedia.

**Statistics:** *State and City Populations*, U.S. Census Bureau, July 1, 2015 estimates; *Land and Water Area*, U.S. Census Bureau, 2010 Census, MAF/TIGER database; *State Temperature Extremes*, NOAA National Climatic Data Center; *Climatology and Average Annual Precipitation*, NOAA National Climatic Data Center, 1980-2015 statewide averages; *State Highest and Lowest Points*, NOAA National Geodetic Survey.

**Websites:** To learn more about the United States, visit booklinks.abdopublishing.com. These links are routinely monitored and updated to provide the most current information available.

### Cataloging-in-Publication Data

Names: Hamilton, John, 1959- author.
Title: Oregon / by John Hamilton.
Description: Minneapolis, MN : Abdo Publishing, [2017] | Series: The United
    States of America | Includes index.
Identifiers: LCCN 2015957726 | ISBN 9781680783391 (lib. bdg.) |
    ISBN 9781680774436 (ebook)
Subjects: LCSH: Oregon--Juvenile literature.
Classification: DDC 979.5--dc23
LC record available at http://lccn.loc.gov/2015957726

# CONTENTS

# THE BEAVER STATE

**M**eriwether Lewis and William Clark first visited present-day Oregon in 1805. A few decades later, thousands of pioneers in covered wagons traveled west on the Oregon Trail. They discovered what Native Americans had known for centuries: Oregon is a land of breathtaking natural beauty, abundant farmland, and vast forests of Douglas fir and ponderosa pine. From sandy Pacific Ocean beaches to snow-capped mountains that kiss the sky, Oregon is an outdoor-lover's paradise.

Oregon is also a land of opportunity. Early in its history, fur trappers and traders made fortunes selling the pelts of animals such as beavers. That is why Oregon is nicknamed "The Beaver State." Today, the state continues to attract and support many businesses, from Intel microprocessor chips used in computers to Nike athletic shoes.

*Bikes, cars, and light-rail trains all travel across the double-deck Steel Bridge in Portland, Oregon. Portland is one of the most bike-friendly places in the United States.*

At 620 feet (189 m), Multnomah Falls is the tallest waterfall in Oregon.

# QUICK FACTS

**Name:** The origin of the word "Oregon" is unknown. There are several theories. Many believe it is a Native American word that refers to the Columbia River.

**State Capital:** Salem, population 164,549

**Date of Statehood:** February 14, 1859 (33$^{rd}$ state)

**Population:** 4,028,977 (27$^{th}$-most populous state)

**Area (Total Land and Water):** 98,379 square miles (254,800 sq km), 9$^{th}$-largest state

**Largest City:** Portland, population 632,309

**Nickname:** The Beaver State

**Motto:** *Alis volat propriis* (She flies with her own wings)

**State Bird:** Western Meadowlark

Oregon Grape

**State Flower:** Oregon Grape

**State Rock:** Thunдеregg

**State Tree:** Douglas Fir

Thunderegg

**State Song:** "Oregon, My Oregon"

**Highest Point:** Mount Hood, 11,239 feet (3,426 m)

**Lowest Point:** Pacific Ocean, 0 feet (0 m)

Douglas Fir

**Average July High Temperature:** 81°F (27°C)

**Record High Temperature:** 119°F (48°C), in Pendleton on August 10, 1898

**Average January Low Temperature:** 26°F (-3°C)

Mt. Hood

**Record Low Temperature:** -54°F (-48°C), in Seneca on February 10, 1933

**Average Annual Precipitation:** 33 inches (84 cm)

Pacific Ocean

**Number of U.S. Senators:** 2

Greetings from OREGON

**Number of U.S. Representatives:** 5

**U.S. Postal Service Abbreviation:** OR

# GEOGRAPHY

Oregon is in the Pacific Northwest region. It is the ninth-largest state in the United States. Its land and water area covers 98,379 square miles (254,800 sq km). To the north is the state of Washington. To the east is Idaho. Oregon shares its southern border with Nevada and California. The entire western side of the state borders the Pacific Ocean.

Oregon's land is unique and complex. The terrain has been formed by many overlapping forces, including glaciers, river erosion, and even volcanoes.

The Coast Range is in western Oregon. It runs north and south along most of the Pacific Ocean coast. There are sandy beaches, rocky cliffs, and forests. Moving inland, the region rises sharply to include low mountains with many small lakes.

South of the Coast Range, in the southwestern corner of Oregon, are the Klamath Mountains. Just east of these rugged peaks is the fertile Rogue Valley.

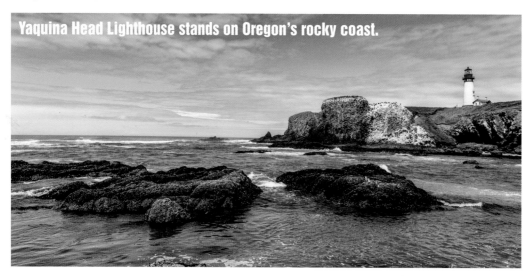

Yaquina Head Lighthouse stands on Oregon's rocky coast.

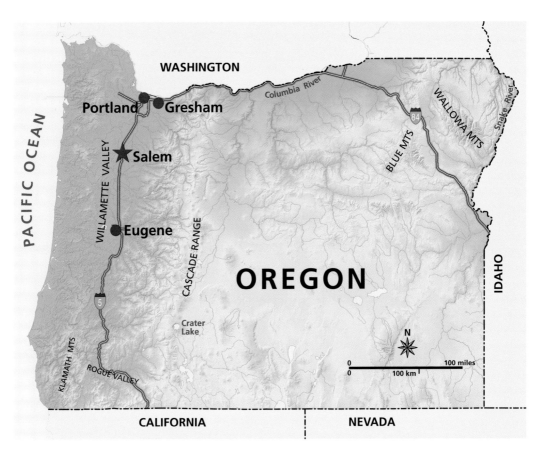

Oregon's total land and water area is
98,379 square miles (254,800 sq km).
It is the 9th-largest state. The state
capital is Salem.

East of the Coast Range is the Willamette Valley. It is a 150-mile (241-km) long valley formed by the Willamette River, which runs from south to north. The soil in the valley is fertile for farming. Most of Oregon's major cities are located in this region.

The Cascade Range is east of the Willamette Valley. These towering mountains run north and south through Oregon. They include a string of tall volcanic peaks. The summit of Mount Hood is the tallest point in Oregon. It soars to 11,239 feet (3,426 m).

The Columbia Plateau is flat and dry. It is east of the Cascade Range, in central and northeastern Oregon. The region was created by volcanoes long ago. There is little rainfall, but the soil is good for irrigation farming. In some areas, there are jagged mountains and deep canyons. The scenic Blue and Wallowa Mountains are in the far northeastern corner of Oregon.

Oregon's southeastern corner is called a high desert. It is part of a larger region called the Basin and Range Province. Only a small amount of rain falls in these semi-arid uplands. The region includes some tall cliffs, hot springs, and salt lakes.

The Willamette Valley's rich soil is perfect for farming.

The Columbia River flows east to west along Oregon's northern border with Washington. Hydroelectric dams on the river provide electricity for homes and businesses. Along Oregon's northeastern border with Idaho is the Snake River. It runs through spectacular Hells Canyon, one of the deepest river gorges in North America. Other important rivers in Oregon include the Deschutes, John Day, and Rogue Rivers. In total, there are more than 112,000 miles (180,247 km) of rivers and streams in the state, and 6,000 lakes.

Rafters travel down the Snake River through Hells Canyon.

# CLIMATE AND
# WEATHER

**M**ost of Oregon has a mild climate. However, there is great variation because of the state's many kinds of landscapes. Along the coast, the weather is usually pleasant throughout the year. Humid air blows in from the Pacific Ocean. The ocean winds result in cool summers and mild winters. There is also much rain in western Oregon, all the way inland to the Cascade Range. The coastal areas average 83 inches (211 cm) of precipitation yearly.

*Strong wind and rain often hit Oregon's coastal areas.*

*Oregon State University students have fun in the snow in Corvallis, Oregon.*

When clouds rise to pass over the tall mountains of the Cascade Range, the moisture condenses and falls as rain or snow. By the time the clouds blow over the mountains, they have little moisture left. This "rain shadow" effect is why eastern Oregon gets much less rain than the rest of the state. Southeastern Oregon on average receives just 13 inches (33 cm) of precipitation each year. Also, far from the moderating ocean winds, the east usually has very hot summers and cold winter temperatures.

Statewide, Oregon averages 33 inches (84 cm) of precipitation yearly. The record high temperature occurred in the town of Pendleton on August 10, 1898, when the thermometer soared to 119°F (48°C). On February 10, 1933, in Seneca, the temperature sank to a bone-chilling record cold of -54°F (-48°C).

**CLIMATE AND WEATHER**

# PLANTS AND
# ANIMALS

Douglas Fir

**D**ense forests cover more than 30.5 million acres (12.3 million ha) of Oregon. That is almost half of the state's land area. There are vast forests of Douglas fir on the rain-drenched western side of the Cascade Range. Douglas fir is the official state tree. It often grows more than 200 feet (61 m) high. It is prized in the logging industry for the amount of usable timber in each tree.

Oregon's largest trees are Sitka spruce. They are found in a narrow strip along the Pacific Ocean coast. Some Sitka spruce reach heights of 300 feet (91 m) or more.

Other trees often found west of the Cascade Range include white fir, pine, redwood, maple, oak, ash, cedar, larch, and mountain hemlock.

*Spring flowers bloom near Oregon's Columbia River Gorge, including purple lupine and yellow arrowleaf balsamroot.*

Ponderosa pine forests grow in the more arid lands east of the Cascade Range. There are also large areas of juniper woodlands. Sagebrush and shrubs such as manzanita grow in the driest part of the state, in the southeast.

Oregon is famed for its more than 1,000 species of wildflowers. They include larkspur, iris, green-tinged paintbrush, red columbine, stream violet, leafy aster, lupine, and yellow arrowleaf balsamroot.

## PLANTS AND ANIMALS

A bobcat prowls through Oregon's Mount Hood National Forest.

Several species of large mammals live in Oregon's forests, plains, and mountains. Elk are found all over the state, but are most numerous in northeastern Oregon, especially in the Blue and Wallowa Mountains. Mule deer live mainly east of the Cascade Range, while white-tailed deer are found in lands west of the mountains. Pronghorn prefer the plains or sagebrush woodlands of eastern Oregon. Mountain goats and bighorn sheep live in the state's mountain regions. Black bears prefer the mountain foothills and western forests.

Other mammals found in Oregon include foxes, porcupines, opossums, bobcats, coyotes, skunks, rabbits, pikas, chipmunks, raccoons, badgers, bats, minks, and river otters. The American beaver is the official state mammal.

Nearly 500 species of birds can be spotted in the skies of Oregon. They include ducks, Canada geese, snow geese, loons, red-winged blackbirds, pelicans, cormorants, quails, pheasants, wild turkeys, sapsuckers, chickadees, finches, woodpeckers, hawks, bald eagles, and owls. The official state bird is the western meadowlark. They have a bold, yellow breast with a black V marking. They like to perch on fences and sing their distinctive flute-like song. Western meadowlarks prefer the arid, open countryside of eastern Oregon, although they can sometimes be found in the Rogue Valley in the southwest.

Fish that swim the lakes, rivers, and Pacific Ocean coast of Oregon include salmon, trout, bass, perch, halibut, catfish, tuna, cod, and smelt.

Along Oregon's coast, many sea creatures thrive, both in the ocean and in tidal pools. Species include sea lions, seals, snails, mussels, crabs, sea stars, turtles, and many kinds of shore birds such as gulls and sandpipers.

*Sea lions make their home along Oregon's Pacific Ocean coast.*

**PLANTS AND ANIMALS**

# HISTORY

Before European explorers arrived in the 1500s, tens of thousands of Native Americans lived in the present-day Oregon area. The first humans came about 15,000 years ago. Over the centuries,

*The Chinook were one of the largest Native American tribes living in Oregon. They used nets to catch salmon in the Columbia River.*

they organized into many groups, or tribes. One of the largest tribes was the Chinook. They built villages along the Columbia River and the Pacific Ocean coast. They caught salmon and other fish for food. Other Native American tribes included the Tillamook, Takelma, Umpqua, Bannock, Chasta, Klamath, and Nez Percé people.

The first Europeans to see Oregon were from Spain. They were sailors traveling along the Pacific Ocean coast, searching for riches in the New World. In 1543, Bartolomé Ferrer led an expedition that spotted the southwestern coast of Oregon.

In 1579, English explorer and privateer Sir Francis Drake may have explored part of Oregon's southern coast. He was trying to find the fabled Northwest Passage, a water route between the Pacific and Atlantic Oceans. Two hundreds years later, British sailor James Cook explored the coast in 1778.

In 1788, Robert Gray, an American sea captain, set foot on the Oregon mainland at Tillamook Bay. In 1792, Gray returned and sailed about 15 miles (24 km) up the Columbia River, naming the river after his ship.

*A statue of Captain Robert Gray stands in front of the Garibaldi Museum in Garibaldi, Oregon. The American sea captain sailed his ship, the* Columbia Rediviva, *up the "Great River of the West," on May 11, 1792.*

In 1805, American explorers Meriwether Lewis and William Clark arrived in Oregon. They came overland from the east. They were the leaders of an expedition called the Corps of Discovery. Sent by President Thomas Jefferson, they were exploring the American West in an effort to find the Northwest Passage. Their travels helped prove that the easy water route between the Atlantic and Pacific Oceans did not exist. However, they did discover the natural resources and beauty of Oregon. The Corps of Discovery spent the winter of 1805-1806 at a wooden stockade they named Fort Clatsop. In the spring, they left for home, where they reported their discoveries.

*The Lewis and Clark Expedition meet members of the Chinook Indian tribe in 1805.*

In 1811, fur trappers backed by businessman John Jacob Astor built a trading post where the Columbia River empties into the Pacific Ocean. The post later became today's city of Astoria. The region became known as Oregon Country, which was much larger than today's state.

During the War of 1812 (1812-1815), Great Britain took control of Astoria. Several years later, in 1818, the United States and Great Britain signed a treaty that gave both countries control of Oregon until a permanent border could be negotiated. The fur trade boomed in the region. People became rich selling beaver pelts, which were prized by European hat makers.

Starting in the 1840s, thousands of American settlers came to Oregon. Beginning their journey in Missouri, the pioneers travelled by covered wagon over a series of old trapper paths and Native American routes that became known as the Oregon Trail. Most of the newcomers settled in the fertile Willamette Valley of western Oregon.

Settlers complete their Oregon Trail journey.

As new pioneers continued to stream into Oregon, it became a United States territory in 1848. Just over 10 years later, it became a state on February 14, 1859. Shortly afterwards, the Civil War (1861-1865) broke out. Oregon remained in the Union rather than join the slave-owning Southern Confederacy.

In the years following the Civil War, Oregon's wood was in high demand all over the country to build houses, furniture, and other products. Railroads were built across Oregon to move logs to factories and sawmills. From there, timber was put on waiting ships at ports along the state's major rivers and ocean coast, to be sent to eager buyers around the country and the world.

The timber industry made Oregon's economy boom in the 1880s and 1890s. Cities grew as more people arrived and started new businesses.

*Logs are ready to float down the Columbia River in 1902.*

*A powerhouse is constructed for the Bonneville Dam on the Columbia River in the late 1930s.*

Oregon was hit hard by the Great Depression of the 1930s, as businesses shut down and people lost their jobs. After World War II (1939-1945), the economy improved. Large hydroelectric dams built on the Columbia River and other waterways provided cheap electricity for Oregon's growing cities.

By the 1960s, Oregonians had serious concerns about the damage done to the state's environment by the logging industry and other big businesses. In the 1970s, lawmakers created rules that forced industries to be more environmentally friendly.

In the 2000s, Oregon continues to attract many businesses to its growing cities. High-technology firms and other businesses have helped make the state less dependent on agriculture and logging.

# DID YOU KNOW?

• Crater Lake National Park contains one of the most beautiful lakes in North America. Located in the Cascade Range, the lake rests atop the remains of an extinct volcano called Mount Mazama. About 7,700 years ago, the volcano erupted and blew its top off, leaving behind a bowl-shaped caldera, or crater. After many centuries of rainfall and melting snow, the caldera filled with water. The surface of the crater is about 6,000 feet (1,829 m) above sea level. It is the deepest lake in the country, plunging to a maximum depth of 1,949 feet (594 m). The lake's deep blue color is a result of its great depth.

• Hells Canyon is one of the deepest river gorges in North America. It is located in the Seven Devils Mountain Range, along the border of Idaho and Oregon. At its deepest point, the canyon wall plummets 7,993 feet (2,436 m) to the Snake River far below, deeper than even Arizona's Grand Canyon.

• Oregon is pronounced "aura-gun," or "ory-gun", but never "or-ee-gone." Some Oregonians get prickly when outsiders mispronounce the state's name. After University of Oregon quarterback Joey Harrington was drafted by the NFL's Detroit Lions in 2002, he passed out "orygun" stickers so television reporters would pronounce his home state properly.

Oregon is pronounced: "Aura-gun" or "Ory-Gun."

• Oregon is the only state that has a flag with a different image on each side. On one side is Oregon's state seal, with the words "State of Oregon 1859" in gold against a navy blue background. On the other side is a gold figure of Oregon's state animal, the beaver, which played a big part in the state's history during the fur-trading days of the 1800s.

**Linus Pauling** (1901-1994) was one of the greatest scientists of the 20th century. He was a chemist, teacher, and peace activist. He developed a synthetic blood plasma for wounded soldiers in World War II. He also worked to unlock the chemical structure of diseases such as sickle-cell anemia. He published more than 850 scientific papers and books. In 1954, he won the Nobel Prize in Chemistry for his work in helping scientists understand the nature of molecules. Pauling was also very concerned about the uncontrolled use and spread of nuclear weapons in the 1950s. He helped bring about a ban of above-ground nuclear bomb testing. For his peace activism, he won a Nobel Peace Prize in 1963. Pauling was born in Portland, Oregon.

**Matt Groening** (1954- ) is a cartoonist, screenwriter, and producer. He is most famous as the creator of the television cartoon series *The Simpsons*, the longest-running, prime-time series in television history. He also created the science fiction cartoon comedy *Futurama*. He has won many honors for his work, including 12 Emmy Awards. Groening was born in Portland, Oregon.

**Beverly Cleary** (1916- ) has sold more than 91 million books worldwide. As a young child, she struggled to read. She became a librarian, and started writing stories about characters children could identify with, including Ramona Quimby, Henry Huggins, and his dog Ribsy. She has won many awards for her work, including the National Book Award and the Newbery Medal. Cleary was born in McMinnville, Oregon.

**James Beard** (1903-1985) was a chef who is often called the father of modern American gourmet cooking. He wrote 20 books that encouraged people to cook with tasty, wholesome food. He loved to teach almost as much as he loved food. He taught cooking at his two schools in New York City, New York, and Seaside, Oregon. He also founded Citymeals-on-Wheels, which helped feed homebound elderly people. Today, the James Beard Foundation continues his message by giving scholarships to people who want to become professional chefs. Each May, the foundation presents the James Beard Awards, honoring the best chefs and restaurants in the country. James Beard was born in Portland, Oregon.

**Abigail Duniway** (1834-1915) was a writer who helped Oregon women gain the right to vote. Born in Illinois, she came to the state in a covered wagon by way of the Oregon Trail. After her farmer husband was injured, she was forced to work to support her family. She eventually started a newspaper called *The New Northwest*, which called for women's rights. Her activism resulted in a 1912 law that gave Oregon women the right to vote.

**Chief Joseph** (1840-1904) was a leader of the Wallowa band of the Nez Percé Native American tribe. He and his people resisted the United States Army's order to move to a reservation. In 1877, the Nez Percé fought skillfully in a long retreat across several states. Finally, Chief Joseph was forced to surrender. "From where the sun now stands," he famously said, "I will fight no more forever." Chief Joseph was born in the Wallowa Valley of northeastern Oregon.

# CITIES

**Portland** is the largest city in Oregon. Its population is about 632,309. It is located in the northern part of the state along the south bank of the Columbia River. Founded in 1845, the city grew as a shipping port for lumber and grain. Today, Portland remains a major port city, but many other businesses help the local economy thrive, including steel, high-technology, and sportswear manufacturers. Portland has a busy arts scene, with many music clubs, symphonies, and operas. There are also dozens of theaters, museums, and fine restaurants and bakeries. Portland has dry summers and cool, rainy winters, which is perfect for growing roses. Portland's nickname is "The City of Roses."

**Salem** is the capital of Oregon. Its population is about 164,549. It is located in the middle of the fertile Willamette Valley. Founded in 1842, it was an agricultural community before becoming the state capital in 1864. Today, there are many government buildings in Salem (government is the number-one employer). There are also many cherry trees, thanks to the climate of western Oregon. Salem's nickname is "The Cherry City." Besides government, other major employers include health care, food processing, lumber, and high-tech manufacturing. There are many historic buildings in Salem. Willamette University was founded in 1842. It is the oldest United States university in the Pacific Northwest.

**Eugene** is located in western Oregon, in the very southern part of the fertile Willamette Valley. Its population is approximately 163,460. Major employers include health care, education, government, and retail. Eugene is famous for its love of outdoor sports, and for supporting the arts. There are dozens of symphonies, choirs, bands, and dance troupes in the city. There are also many live theater groups. The Hult Center for the Performing Arts is in downtown Eugene. It has a theater, two concert halls, and an art gallery. The University of Oregon was established in 1876. It enrolls more than 24,000 students.

The Gresham History Museum was the town's first public library.

**Gresham** is the fourth-largest city in Oregon. Its population is about 110,553. It is located just a few miles east of Portland. Gresham was established in 1905 as a small farming community. Today, it is a fast-growing city known for its many parks and historic sites. The Zimmerman House Museum is in a restored 1874 farmhouse. It has thousands of artifacts from Oregon's pioneer days. The Gresham Arts Festival is held in the city's historic downtown each summer. It features the work of artists from all over Oregon and southern Washington. Just minutes east of Gresham is the breathtaking, 80-mile (129-km) -long Columbia River Gorge National Scenic Area.

# TRANSPORTATION

Oregon has 71,228 miles (114,630 km) of public roadways. Interstate I-5 runs north and south through the western part of the state, including the Willamette Valley, where most of Oregon's largest cities are located. Interstate I-84 runs generally east and west. Starting in Portland, it closely follows the Columbia River before turning southeast and exiting the state at the Idaho border.

There are several large ports in Oregon where cargo can be loaded onto ocean-going ships. Port of Portland, which is situated along the deep Columbia River, is the busiest marine terminal. It handles more than 12 million tons (10.9 million metric tons) of bulk cargo each year, including cars, grains, and minerals. There are several other ports along the Columbia, Snake, and Willamette Rivers. Oregon also has 14 coastal ports, including deepwater ports in Newport and Coos Bay.

*A container ship is loaded at the Port of Portland's Terminal 6. The busy port is situated along the Columbia River.*

*Portland International Airport handles nearly 17 million passengers yearly.*

There are 18 freight railroads in Oregon operating on 2,396 miles (3,856 km) of track. The most common items hauled by rail include lumber and wood products, paper and pulp, automobiles, chemicals, farm products, and coal. Amtrak provides passenger service on its Coast Starlight, Amtrak Cascades, and Empire Builder lines.

Oregon's busiest airport is Portland International Airport. It handles nearly 17 million passengers yearly.

## TRANSPORTATION

# NATURAL
# RESOURCES

There are 34,600 farms and ranches in Oregon, operating on 16.4 million acres (6.6 million ha) of land. That is about one-quarter of the state's total land area. The most valuable crops include hay, wheat, potatoes, onions, mint, sweet corn, strawberries, beans, cherries, apples, sugar beets, garlic, and grapes. Oregon grows 99 percent of the nation's hazelnuts. It is the state's official nut. The pear is Oregon's official state fruit.

There are many cattle ranches in the eastern part of Oregon, where there is plenty of open rangeland. Other important livestock products include poultry and eggs, milk from dairy farming, plus sheep and hogs.

*Oregon grows 99 percent of the nation's hazelnuts.*

*Oregon's logging and saw mill operations utilize the state's plentiful forestlands.*

Rivers are one of Oregon's most important natural resources. Huge hydroelectric dams, such as those on the Columbia and Snake Rivers, provide cheap electricity for the state's residents and businesses. Oregon also has many wind turbines and solar power plants. In total, the state generates nearly 75 percent of its power needs from renewable energy sources.

Dense forests cover almost half of Oregon's land area. The state leads the nation in softwood lumber production. It is also the nation's top-ranked Christmas tree producer.

Off Oregon's Pacific Ocean coast, the commercial fishing industry hauls in big catches of salmon, tuna, halibut, crab, and many other species.

Most of Oregon's mining industry produces gravel and crushed stone. It also extracts pumice, perlite, talc, and bentonite.

## NATURAL RESOURCES

# INDUSTRY

In recent decades, Oregon's economy has made a big shift from logging and agriculture to manufacturing, especially high-technology companies. Businesses like to locate where it is easy to ship raw materials and finished goods, and where there is an educated workforce that enjoys a high quality of life. Oregon has all of these advantages.

There are many high-technology companies in Oregon that manufacture and sell computers or computer-related products. Many of them are grouped in Portland and the surrounding area, in a region called the Silicon Forest. Intel, a major maker of semiconductor computer chips, is Oregon's largest private employer. Other high-tech companies that have facilities in the area include eBay, IBM, Microsoft, and Hewlett-Packard.

*Intel is Oregon's largest private employer. The high-tech company expanded its Hillsboro, Oregon, location in 2015.*

*The sprawling Nike World Headquarters is in Beaverton, Oregon.*

There are many other kinds of manufacturers in Oregon besides high-tech. Beaverton is the headquarters of Nike, Inc., the shoe and sporting-goods manufacturing giant. Cofounded in 1964 by University of Oregon track-and-field coach Bill Bowerman and former athlete and businessman Phil Knight, Nike today is one of the most profitable and recognizable brands in sports.

Many Oregon workers are employed in the service industry, which includes health care, insurance, advertising, financial services, and marketing. Tourism is very important to Oregon's economy. In recent years, visitors have spent almost $11 billion in the state, supporting more than 105,000 jobs.

## INDUSTRY

# SPORTS

The Portland Trail Blazers are a major league basketball team. They play in the National Basketball Association (NBA). In 1977, the team won its first national championship. They have appeared in the NBA Finals several times.

The Portland Timbers are a Major League Soccer (MLS) team. It won its first MLS Cup championship in 2015. The Portland Thorns FC play in the National Women's Soccer League (NWSL). The team won the first NWSL championship at the end of the inaugural 2013 season.

College sports are closely followed in Oregon. Teams from the University of Oregon, in Eugene, are called the Oregon Ducks. There are 18 varsity men's and women's teams. Football and track & field are especially popular. Teams from Oregon State University, in Corvallis, are called the Beavers. Students compete on 17 men's and women's teams. Competition between the Beavers and Ducks men's football teams is one of the longest-running rivalries in college sports.

Outdoor sports are an important part of Oregon life. The state is an angler's paradise. Biking, kayaking, and hiking are also popular. Each year, more than 10,000 people attempt to reach the summit of Mount Hood, Oregon's tallest peak, which rises 11,239 feet (3,426 m).

People hike near Mount Hood.

41

# ENTERTAINMENT

Oregon has hundreds of museums, art galleries, live theaters, bands, orchestras, and historical sites to explore. The Portland Art Museum is one of the largest art museums in the country. In its collections are more than 42,000 pieces of fine art, ranging from modern American and European art to masterpieces of Native American and Asian cultures.

The Oregon Museum of Science and Industry is located in Portland. It features a planetarium and exhibition halls dedicated to science and natural history. Visitors can also tour the USS *Blueback*, a United States Navy submarine that appeared in the film *The Hunt for Red October*. The *Blueback* is docked at a pier on the Willamette River next to the museum.

*The Oregon Museum of Science and Industry (OMSI) is located in Portland, Oregon. The popular museum features space, fossil, ocean, agriculture, and renewable energy exhibits, as well as tours of the USS* Blueback *submarine.*

*McMinnville's Evergreen Aviation & Space Museum features the Hughes H-4 Hercules flying boat. Because aluminum was in such short supply during World War II, the plane was made mostly of wood. It is nicknamed the* Spruce Goose, *although it is actually made almost entirely of birch.*

The Columbia River Gorge National Scenic Area is an 80-mile (129-km) -long section of a wide canyon carved by the Columbia River. There are many hiking and mountain biking trails to explore. The spectacular scenery includes dozens of waterfalls. World-famous Multnomah Falls is 620 feet (189 m) high.

At the Evergreen Aviation & Space Museum in McMinnville, visitors can see more than 20 vintage military and civilian aircraft, including the huge wooden aircraft the *Spruce Goose*, built by billionaire aviator Howard Hughes.

At the John Day Fossil Beds National Monument's three units in northeastern Oregon, visitors can see fossils that are more than 50 million years old.

**ENTERTAINMENT**

# TIMELINE

**13,000 BC**—The first humans arrive in present-day Oregon.

**1543**—Bartolomé Ferrer of Spain sails along Oregon's southwestern coast.

**1579**—English explorer Francis Drake explores Oregon's coast.

**1788**—American sea captain Robert Gray sets foot on Oregon soil at Tillamook Bay.

**1792**—Robert Gray returns to Oregon and sails several miles up the Columbia River, naming the river after his ship.

**1805**—Lewis and Clark reach Oregon overland from the east. They spend the winter at Fort Clatsop near the Pacific Ocean.

**1811**—The first European settlement in Oregon is founded. The fur trading post later becomes the city of Astoria.

**1840s**—The first waves of pioneers arrive after traveling by covered wagon along the Oregon Trail.

**1848**—Oregon becomes a territory of the United States.

**1859**—Oregon becomes the 33rd state in the Union.

**1884**—Travel between Oregon and the rest of the United States by train becomes possible.

**1937**—Construction is completed on the Bonneville Dam, a hydroelectric dam on the Columbia River.

**1960s and 1970s**—Oregon becomes a pioneer in the environmental movement.

**2002**—A lightning strike sets off the Sour Biscuit Fire, scorching more than 500,000 acres (202,343 ha) in southern Oregon and northern California.

**2015**—The Portland Timbers soccer team wins the MLS Cup championship.

# GLOSSARY

**Chinook**

A Native American tribe that lived along the coast of the Pacific Ocean and along the banks of the Columbia River. The Chinook were known for their skills in building canoes and fishing.

**Fur Trapper**

A person who catches animals for their soft, thick coats of hair, which are later made into clothing such as coats or hats.

**Gourmet**

A person who likes very good-tasting food that is specially prepared.

**Kayak**

An enclosed canoe with a small opening in the center of the top. A pole with paddles at each end is used to move the kayak through the water.

**Molecules**

One or more atoms joined together in a group. An atom is a tiny particle that is like a building block. In water, for example, two hydrogen atoms combine with an oxygen atom ($H_2O$) to create one water molecule.

**New World**

The areas of North, Central, and South America, as well as islands near these land masses. The term was often used by European explorers.

### Nobel Prize

A prize given annually to recognize advances in science and culture. The prizes are given in several categories, such as chemistry, medicine, literature, and peace. The Nobel Prize is considered by many to be the most prestigious award in the world. It is named after Alfred Nobel, a Swedish inventor.

### Northwest Passage

A water passage that Europeans hoped to find that linked the Atlantic Ocean to the Pacific Ocean.

### Sawmill

A place that cuts logs into lumber.

### Spruce Goose

A huge "flying boat" created by aviator Howard Hughes during World War II. Also called the Hughes H-4 Hercules, it was hoped that the big plane could transport war materials. Because there was so little metal available during wartime, the ship was built out of wood, although mostly birch (not spruce, as the nickname implies). Weighing 300,000 pounds (136,078 kg), and with a wingspan of 320 feet (98 m), it became one of the biggest airplanes ever built. Hughes flew the plane only once, on November 2, 1947. Today, the plane is in the Evergreen Aviation & Space Museum in McMinnville, Oregon.

### World War II

A conflict that was fought from 1939 to 1945, involving countries around the world. The United States entered the war after Japan bombed the American naval base at Pearl Harbor, in Oahu, Hawaii, on December 7, 1941.

# INDEX